Practical Pre-School Books

Planning for Learning through
The Sea

by Rachel Sparks Linfield Illustrated by Cathy Hughes

Contents

Published by Step Forward Publishing Limited

St Jude's Church, Dulwich Road, Herne Hill, London, SE24 0PB Tel. 020 7738 5454

© Step Forward Publishing Limited 2009

www.practicalpreschoolbooks.com

Planning for Learning through The Sea ISBN: 978 1 90457 560 3

Making plans

Why plan?

The purpose of planning is to make sure that all children enjoy a broad and balanced curriculum. All planning should be useful. Plans are working documents that you spend time preparing, which later should repay your efforts. Try to be concise. This will help you to find information quickly when you need it.

Long-term plans

Preparing a long-term plan, which maps out the curriculum during a year or even two, will help you to ensure that you are providing a variety of activities and are meeting the *Statutory Framework for the Early Years Foundation Stage* (2007).

Your long-term plan need not be detailed. Divide the time period over which you are planning into fairly equal sections such as half terms. Choose a topic for each section. Young children benefit from making links between the new ideas they encounter so as you select each topic, think about the time of year in which you

plan to do it. A topic about minibeasts will not be very successful in November!

Although each topic will address all the learning areas, some could focus on a specific area. For example, a topic on the sea would lend itself well to activities relating to Knowledge and Understanding of the World and Creative Development. Another topic might particularly encourage the appreciation of stories. Try to make sure that you provide a variety of topics in your long-term plans such as:

Autumn 1	Nursery Rhymes
Autumn 2	Autumn/Christmas
Spring 1	Weather
Spring 2	Shopping
Summer 1	Recycling
Summer 2	The Sea

Medium-term plans

Medium-term plans will outline the contents of a topic in a little more detail. One way to start this process is by brainstorming on a large piece of paper. Work with your team writing down all the activities you can think of which are relevant to the topic. As you do this it may become clear that some activities go well together. Think about dividing them into themes. The topic of 'the Sea', for example, has themes such as 'Sea detectives', 'Sand, shells and pebbles', 'On the sea', Sea creatures and plants', 'Sea and beach safety' and the 'Beach party'.

At this stage it is helpful to make a chart. Write the theme ideas down the side of the chart and put a different area of learning at the top of each column. Now you can insert your brainstormed ideas and will quickly see where there are gaps. As you complete the chart take account of children's earlier experiences and provide opportunities for them to progress.

Refer back to the *Statutory Framework for the Early Years Foundation Stage* and check that you have addressed as many different aspects of it as you can. Once all your medium-term plans are complete make sure that there are no neglected areas.

Making plans

Day-to-day plans

The plans you make for each day will outline aspects such as:

- resources needed;
- the way in which you might introduce activities;
- individual needs;
- the organisation of adult help;
- size of the group;
- timing;
- safety;
- key vocabulary.

Identify the learning and the ELGs that each activity is intended to promote. Make a note of any assessments or observations that you are likely to carry out. After carrying out the activities, make notes on your plans to say what was particularly successful, or any changes you would make another time.

A final note

Planning should be seen as flexible. Not all groups meet every day, and not all children attend every day. Any part of the plan can be used independently, stretched over a longer period or condensed to meet the needs of any group. You will almost certainly adapt the activities as children respond to them in different ways and bring their own ideas, interests and enthusiasms. The important thing is to ensure that the children are provided with a varied and enjoyable curriculum that meets their individual developing needs.

Using the book

- Collect or prepare suggested resources as listed on page 21.
- Read the section which outlines links to the Early Learning Goals (pages 4 - 7) and explains the rationale for the topic 'the Sea'.
- For each weekly theme two activities are described in detail as an example to help you in your planning

and preparation. Key vocabulary, questions and learning opportunities are identified.

- The skills overview of the six-week plan, on page 23, will help you to see at a glance which aspects of children's development are being addressed as a focus each week.
- As children take part in the topic activities, their learning will progress. Collecting Evidence on page 22 explains how you might monitor children's achievements.
- Find out on page 20 how the topic can be brought together in a beach party to involve carers, children and friends.

There is additional material to support the working partnership of families and children in the form of a Home Links page, and a photocopiable Parent Page found at the back of the book.

It is important to appreciate that the ideas presented in this book will only be a part of your planning. Many activities that will be taking place as routine in your group may not be mentioned. For example, it is assumed that sand, dough, water, puzzles, floor toys and large scale apparatus are part of the ongoing early years experience, as are the opportunities for children to develop ICT skills. Role-play areas, stories, rhymes, singing, and group discussion times are similarly assumed to be happening in each week although they may not be a focus for described activities. Groups should also ensure that there is a balance of adult-led and child-initiated activities.

Using the 'Early Learning Goals'

Having chosen your topic and made your medium-term plans you can use the Statutory Framework for the Early Years Foundation Stage to highlight the key learning opportunities your activities will address. The Early Learning Goals are split into six areas: Personal, Social and Emotional Development; Communication, Language and Literacy; Problem Solving, Reasoning and Numeracy; Knowledge and Understanding of the World; Physical Development and Creative Development. Do not expect each of your topics to cover every goal but your long-term plans should allow for all of them to be addressed by the time a child enters Year 1.

The following section gives the Early Learning Goals in point form to show what children are expected to be able to do in each area of learning by the time they enter Year 1. These points will be used throughout this book to show how activities for a topic on 'the Sea' link to these expectations. For example Personal, Social and Emotional Development point 7 is 'form good relationships with adults and peers'. Activities suggested which provide the opportunity for children to do this will have the reference PS7. This will enable you to see which parts of the Early Learning Goals are covered in a given week and to plan for areas to be revisited and developed.

In addition you can ensure that activities offer variety in the goals to be encountered. Often an activity may be carried out to work towards different Early Learning Goals. For instance, during this topic children will make grass (hula) skirts from ribbon and crepe paper. They will have the opportunity to develop personal skills as they select resources independently. In addition, there will be creative development as they make choices about colours, and wear the skirts to dance. It is important, therefore, that activities have clearly defined goals so that these may be emphasised during the activity and for recording purposes.

Personal, Social and Emotional Development (PS)

This area of learning covers important aspects of development that affect the way children learn, behave and relate to others. By the end of the Early Years Foundation Stage (EYFS) children should:

PS1 Continue to be interested, excited and motivated to learn.

PS2 Be confident to try new activities, initiate ideas and speak in a familiar group.

PS3 Maintain attention, concentrate, and sit quietly when appropriate.

PS4 Respond to significant experiences, showing a range of feelings when appropriate.

PS5 Have a developing awareness of their own needs, views and feelings, and be sensitive to the needs, views and feelings of others.

PS6 Have a developing respect for their own cultures and beliefs and those of other people.

PS7 Form good relationships with adults and peers.

PS8 Work as a part of a group or class, taking turns and sharing fairly, understanding that there needs to be agreed values and codes of behaviour for groups of people, including adults and children, to work together harmoniously.

PS9 Understand what is right, what is wrong and why.

PS10 Consider the consequences of their words and actions for themselves and others.

PS11 Dress and undress independently and manage their own personal hygiene.

PS12 Select and use activities and resources independently.

PS13 Understand that people have different needs, views, cultures and beliefs, that need to be treated with respect.

PS14 Understand that they can expect others to treat their needs, views, cultures and beliefs with respect.

The topic, 'the Sea' offers many opportunities for children's personal, social and emotional development. Times spent discussing facts about the sea, sand and pebbles and the role of lifeguards will encourage the children to be interested and motivated to learn. Learning about sun safety will help the children to consider consequences and understand what is wrong, what is right and why. Many of the areas outlined above, though, will be covered on an almost incidental basis as children carry out the activities described in this book for the other areas of children's learning. During undirected free time they will be developing PS12, whilst any small group activity that involves working with an adult will help children to work towards PS7.

Communication, Language and Literacy (L)

By the end of the EYFS, children should:

L1 Interact with others, negotiating plans and activities and taking turns in conversation.

L2 Enjoy listening to and using spoken and written language, and readily turn to it in their play and learning.

L3 Sustain attentive listening, responding to what they have heard with relevant comments, questions or actions.

L4 Listen with enjoyment, and respond to stories, songs and other music, rhymes and poems and make up their own stories, songs, rhymes and poems.

L5 Extend their vocabulary, exploring the meanings and sounds of new words.

L6 Speak clearly and audibly with confidence and control and show awareness of the listener.

L7 Use language to imagine and recreate roles and experiences.

L8 Use talk to organise, sequence and clarify thinking, ideas, feelings and events.

L9 Hear and say sounds in words in the order in which they occur.

L10 Link sounds to letters, naming and sounding the letters of the alphabet.

L11 Use their phonic knowledge to write simple regular words and make phonetically plausible attempts at more complex words.

L12 Explore and experiment with sounds, words and texts.

L13 Retell narratives in the correct sequence, drawing on language patterns of stories.

L14 Read a range of familiar and common words and simple sentences independently.

L15 Know that print carries meaning and, in English, is read from left to right and top to bottom.

L16 Show an understanding of the elements of stories, such as main character, sequence of events and openings, and how information can be found in non-fiction texts to answer questions about where, who, why and how.

L17 Attempt writing for different purposes, using features of different forms such as lists, stories and instructions.

L18 Write their own names and other things such as labels and captions, and begin to form simple sentences, sometimes using punctuation.

L19 Use a pencil and hold it effectively to form recognisable letters, most of which are correctly formed.

A number of the activities suggested for the theme 'the Sea' encourage the children to write using their phonic knowledge and to recognise words. They have the opportunity to produce posters, write recipes and make beach party tickets. Activities using fiction, allow the children to enjoy sharing books and to respond in a variety of ways to what they hear, reinforcing and extending their vocabularies. Throughout all the activities the children should be encouraged to interact and to listen.

Problem Solving, Reasoning and Numeracy (N)

By the end of the EYFS, children should:

N1 Say and use number names in order in familiar contexts.

N2 Count reliably up to ten everyday objects.

N3 Recognise numerals 1 to 9.

N4 Use developing mathematical ideas and methods to solve practical problems.

N5   In practical activities and discussion, begin to use the vocabulary involved in adding and subtracting.

N6   Use language such as 'more' or 'less' to compare two numbers.

N7   Find one more or one less than a number from one to ten.

N8   Begin to relate addition to combining two groups of objects and subtraction to 'taking away'.

N9   Use language such as 'greater', 'smaller', 'heavier' or 'lighter' to compare quantities.

N10   Talk about, recognise and recreate simple patterns.

N11   Use language such as 'circle' or 'bigger' to describe the shape and size of solids and flat shapes.

N12   Use everyday words to describe position.

The theme 'the Sea' provides a meaningful context for activities that encourage the children to use numbers, to reason and to solve problems. The opportunity to count occurs as children use the 'Surf number rhyme' and count pebbles. Children will explore shapes and size as they make collages of boats. Children will recognise and create patterns as they make lifeguard flags. The use of positional language is encouraged in a role-play sea.

Knowledge and Understanding of the World (K)

By the end of the EYFS, children should:

K1   Investigate objects and materials by using all of their senses as appropriate.

K2   Find out about, and identify, some features of living things, objects and events they observe.

K3   Look closely at similarities, differences, patterns and change.

K4   Ask questions about why things happen and how things work.

K5   Build and construct with a wide range of objects, selecting appropriate resources and adapting their work where necessary.

K6   Select the tools and techniques they need to shape, assemble and join materials they are using.

K7   Find out about and identify the uses of everyday technology and use information and communication technology and programmable toys to support their learning.

K8   Find out about past and present events in their own lives, and in those of their families and other people they know.

K9   Observe, find out about and identify features in the place they live and the natural world.

K10   Find out about their environment, and talk about those features they like and dislike.

K11   Begin to know about their own cultures and beliefs and those of other people.

The topic of 'the Sea' offers opportunities for children to make observations, and to compare. As they explore beach shoes and shells the children are encouraged to notice details. Activities such as making paper plate fish and models of beach shoes give them the opportunity to select materials and to construct. Through all the activities children should be encouraged to observe, to talk and to give reasons for choices and observations.

Physical Development (PD)

By the end of the EYFS, children should:

PD1   Move with confidence, imagination and in safety.

PD2   Move with control and coordination.

PD3   Travel around, under, over and through balancing and climbing equipment.

PD4   Show awareness of space, of themselves and of others.

PD5   Recognise the importance of keeping healthy, and those things which contribute to this.

PD6   Recognise the changes that happen to their bodies when they are active.

PD7   Use a range of small and large equipment.

PD8   Handle tools, objects, construction and malleable materials safely and with increasing control.

Activities such as making shell prints in playdough will offer experience of the ELG PD8. Through pretending to surf and to go on a beach walk children will have the opportunity to move with control and imagination. When playing traditional beach games and using a range of small equipment the children will be encouraged to develop their co-ordination.

Creative Development (C)

By the end of the EYFS, children should:

C1   Respond in a variety of ways to what they see, hear, smell, touch and feel.

C2   Express and communicate their ideas, thoughts and feelings by using a widening range of materials, suitable tools, imaginative and role-play, movement, designing and making, and a variety of songs and musical instruments.

C3   Explore colour, texture, shape, form and space in two or three dimensions.

C4   Recognise and explore how sounds can be changed, sing simple songs from memory, recognise repeated sounds and sound patterns and match movements to music.

C5   Use their imagination in art and design, music, dance, imaginative and role-play and stories.

During this topic children will experience working with a variety of materials as they make paper plate sun hats and sea creatures, decorate T-shirts and felt fish. They will be able to develop their imaginations and skills of painting, drawing and colouring as they create posters and pictures of the sea. Throughout all the activities children should be encouraged to talk about what they see and feel as they communicate their ideas in painting, models, collage work and role-play. When singing songs about the sea the children will recognise and explore how sounds can be changed.

Week 1
Sea detectives

Personal, Social and Emotional Development

- Show the children pictures of the sea. Talk about what the sea is and the kinds of things that people do in the sea. If any of the children have been to the seaside, ask them to describe what they saw and did. (PS3, 7)
- Look at a globe. Show the children where they live. Help them to realise how much of the world is covered by sea. Link to the activity opposite. (PS1, 2)
- Earth finger painting (see activity opposite). (PS1, 2)

Communication, Language and Literacy

- Show the children how to write the word 'sea'. As a group, make a collection of words that rhyme with 'sea'. Write each word on a piece of card and place them in a bucket. Investigate how many words can be read before the sand runs through a timer. (L2)
- Involve the children in making a collection of non-fiction and fiction books about the sea. Enjoy sharing the books. (L16)
- Make seaside postcards by cutting pictures from travel brochures. Encourage the children to imagine that they are on holiday by the sea and to enjoy 'writing' postcards. (L11, 18, 19)

Problem Solving, Reasoning and Numeracy

- Use a collection of seaside postcards for sorting and counting activities. (N1, 2)
- Use a blue sheet as the sea. Involve the children in making a seaside display of shells, plastic fish, seaweed cut from paper etc. Use positional language to instruct the children where, initially, to place the objects. Play 'I spy a … that is …' using positional and size vocabulary within the clues. (N11, 12)

Knowledge and Understanding of the World

- Talk about the fact that sea water is salty. Leave either real sea water or water mixed with salt in a shallow, plastic container in a warm place. Each day look at the container, and as the water evaporates talk to the children about what is happening and why salt crystals appear. (K9)
- Show the children pictures of the Dead Sea. Talk about why it is special and how things float easily in such salty water. (K9)
- On unwanted CDs stick pictures of things found in the sea. Encourage the children to use correct words to describe the things they choose. Hang the discs up and enjoy investigating how they reflect light. (K1)

Physical Development

- Outside, draw wavy lines with chalk. Challenge the children to move along the lines in different ways. (PD1, 2)
- Tap or dribble balls along the wavy lines. (PD2, 7)
- Encourage the children to mime paddling, jumping waves, swimming in the sea and drying with towels. Do some of the activities quickly so that the children can notice how their bodies change when they are active. (PD1, 6)

Creative Development

- Use pastels, chalks or paint to make pictures of the sea. (C3)
- Magazine collages (see activity opposite). (C3)

Activity: Earth finger painting

Learning opportunity: Gaining understanding that much of the earth is covered by sea. Using finger paint to make seas.

Early learning goal: Personal, Social and Emotional Development. Children should continue to be interested, excited and motivated to learn. They should be confident to try new activities, initiate ideas and speak in a familiar group.

Resources: A world globe, saucer-sized circles of green sugar paper; blue finger paint.

Key vocabulary: Sea, land, world, globe, blue, green.

Organisation: Small groups.

What to do: Show the group a world globe and point out where they live. Encourage the children to look at the globe and to say what they notice. Point to different features such as land and sea. Help the children to realise that a large proportion is covered by sea.

Show the group the paper circles. Demonstrate how to put finger paint onto a circle as sea leaving areas of green to be land. Compare the finger painted circle with the globe. Give each child a circle to make their own planet earths with sea and land.

Activity: Magazine collages

Learning opportunity: Making collages and realising that there are many shades and tones of blue.

Early learning goal: Creative Development. Children should explore colour, texture, shape, form and space in two or three dimensions

Resources: Collection of colour supplements and magazines; PVA glue, scissors, black sugar paper; pictures of seas and beaches; postcard-sized pieces of card.

Key vocabulary: Blue, different, similar, sea, wave, sky.

Organisation: Small groups.

What to do: Show the children the pictures of the sea and beaches. Pick a picture and ask the children to look through a magazine to find a piece of blue that is the same as a bit in the picture. Encourage them to notice the different shades of blue. Explain that they are going to make pictures of the sea using strips of blue cut or torn from magazines.

As a group make a collection of pieces of blue cut from the magazines. Demonstrate how to glue overlapping strips of magazine, onto the card, to give the effect of sky, sea and clouds. When the pictures are complete add a silhouette of a boat or fish cut from black sugar paper. Finish by varnishing the pictures with watered down PVA glue.

Display

Cover all the boards in the setting with sea coloured wallpaper to create a watery feeling. Put up a variety of blue borders such as wavy lines, circles as bubbles and cut-out lower case letters for a phonics display. Ask the children to bring in postcards and photos of places by the sea for one display. Put up the sea pictures on another board with name labels and titles done by the children. Double mount the magazine collages and display them with questions and prompts of things for which to search. Hang the CDs at varying heights to represent bubbles made by fish. Intersperse the CDs with seaweed made from strips of blue and green crepe paper.

Week 2
Sand, shells and pebbles

Personal, Social and Emotional Development
- Talk about how sand is formed by the sea wearing away rocks. Use plastic magnifiers to examine sand. (PS1)
- Enjoy examining a range of shells and pebbles. Describe the textures and colours. Ask the children to pick their favourite pebbles and shells. Encourage the children to talk about their likes and dislikes. (PS4, 5)

Communication, Language and Literacy
- In the sand tray enjoy practising letter formation. (L19)
- Sand, pebble and shell feeling poems (see activity opposite). (L3, 4)

Problem Solving, Reasoning and Numeracy
- Use A5 paper, tape and straws to make flags for sandcastles. Decorate the flags with 2-D shapes or repeated patterns of stripes and spots. Encourage the children to talk about the patterns, colours and shapes that they use. (N10, 11)
- Use pebbles and buckets for counting activities. (N1, 2)
- Sort shells into hoops by colour, size and type. Encourage the children to work out how many more shells there are in one hoop than another. (N1, 5, 6)

Knowledge and Understanding of the World
- Compare the differences between wet and dry sand. What type of sand is best for making sand castles? Why? (K3)
- Make close observational drawings of shells. Talk about the colours, shapes and patterns. (K1, 3)

Physical Development
- Use sand timers to encourage the children to perform a given action in a certain time. Challenges could include activities such as throwing beanbags into a bucket, catching and throwing balls and jumping on the spot. (PD7)
- Explore the patterns made by pressing shells into play-dough or clay. (PD8)

Creative Development
- Use coloured sands to make pictures of fish. (C3)
- Make a sea picture by sticking sand, shells and small stones on a piece of stiff, blue card. Use lolly sticks to give it a frame. (C3)
- Pebble Paperweights (see activity opposite). (C3)

Activity: Sand, pebble and shell feeling poems

Learning opportunity: Collaborating to make up a 'feeling poem'.

Early learning goal: Communication, Language and Literacy. Children should sustain attentive listening, responding to what they have heard with relevant comments, questions or actions. They should ... make up their own ... rhymes and poems.

Resources: Sand tray with a collection of buried shells and safe-sized pebbles, flip chart and pen.

Key vocabulary: Sand, sea, pebble, shell, words to describe feelings.

Organisation: Groups of 3 children.

What to do: Gather around the sand tray. Invite a child to put their hand in the sand and describe how it feels. On the flip chart write:

My hand,
Is in the sand.

The sand feels …

Encourage the children to suggest words to complete the first verse of the group poem and write down the ideas.

Invite another child to investigate the sand and find a pebble. Ask for words to describe how the pebble feels and again write their ideas down to make a second verse:

My hand,
Is in the sand.
And finds a pebble
The pebble feels …

Finish by finding the shell. On further occasions poems could describe how the objects look.

Activity: Pebble paperweights

Learning opportunity: Gaining awareness of what pebbles are and using pebbles to make paperweights.

Early learning goal: Creative Development. Children should explore colour, texture, shape, form and space in two or three dimensions.

Resources: Smooth, egg-sized pebbles, paint, thin brushes, an example of a bought paperweight, felt-pens, glue, decorative materials.

Key vocabulary: Pebble, stone, paperweight, names for colours and patterns.

Organisation: Small groups.

What to do: Show the children a paperweight. Explain that paperweights can be used to stop pieces of paper from blowing away from a table. Put out a selection of pebbles for the group to feel. Talk about where the pebbles were found. Encourage the children to describe their textures. Explain that some pebbles are smooth because the rock has gradually been worn away by the sea and rain.

Ask each child to choose a pebble that they think would make a good paperweight and to give reasons for their choices. Tell the group that they can use paint, felt pens or glue and scrap materials to decorate their pebbles to be paperweights. Invite suggestions for ways to change their pebbles such as patterns or to be a creature such as a bee or ladybird.

Display

Cover two tables with blue paper or fabric. On one table set out the paperweights with a 'please look with your eyes' sign and name labels made by the children. On the second table put out non-fiction book showing shells, a collection of shells to sort and a bowl of sand to examine with plastic magnifiers. Nearby, display the drawings of shells with labels to show their type.

Week 3
On the sea

Personal, Social and Emotional Development

- Set out small stools or chairs to be a boat. Invite children to enjoy role-play as sailors. Encourage them to look for sea creatures, to remain seated whilst out 'on the water' and to consider why they need to take care whilst in a boat. (PS10)
- Use books to find pictures of the way that the types and shapes of boats have changed over time. Encourage the children to think about what the boats would be like to travel in. (PS1, 4)

Communication, Language and Literacy

- Write a group story that starts with the line 'From my boat on the sea, I can see…' Encourage the children to think of views and sea creatures. Scribe the story with the children helping to spell words. (L4)
- Look at the words 'see' and 'sea'. Find other common words that sound the same but are spelt differently. (L9, 11)
- Making letter waves (see activity opposite). (L19)

Problem Solving, Reasoning and Numeracy

- Talk about tides, high tide and low tide. Talk about the meanings of the words 'high' and 'low'. Play a game in which a small, toy boat is hidden for the children to find following clues using positional language. On further occasions let the children take turns to do the hiding and the providing of the clues. (N12)
- As a group make a large picture of the sea. Use positional language to explain to the children where to draw or stick boats, people and fish. (N12)
- Surfboard number rhymes (see activity opposite). (N1, 2, 8)

Knowledge and Understanding of the World

- Use a water tray or washing up bowls half filled with water to investigate what will float. Help the children to realise that objects will float if 'they are light for their size' (e.g a marble sinks, a dinghy floats.). (K4)
- Make rafts from lolly sticks held together with elastic bands. Investigate how well they float. How many 2 pence coins can they balance before they sink? (K5)

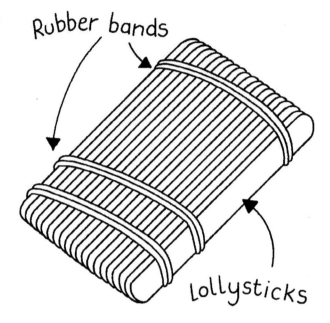

Lollystick rafts

Rubber bands

Lollysticks

- Provide a range of materials (e.g. plastic lids, polystyrene trays, wood pieces, etc.) for children to use to make boats, surfboards and rafts. (K5, 6)

Physical Development

- Explain that people who ride the waves on surfboards have to be good at balancing. Provide opportunities for the children to balance such as walking along benches and chalked lines and standing on one leg. (PD2, 3)
- Tell a story of going for a surf session. Encourage the children to stretch and balance as they pretend to surf. (PD1, 2, 4)

Creative Development

- Enjoy singing sea shanties. (C4)
- Make sea tiles by sticking pieces of sea coloured tissue papers on a square of stiff card. Varnish the tiles with watered down PVA glue. (C3)
- Make up sea dances. Encourage the children to move like waves, rolling up a beach and then gracefully going back towards the horizon. (C5)
- On white circles of paper (portholes), paint pictures of the views described in the group poem (see Communication Language and Literacy). (C3)

Making letter waves

W W W W W W W W W W

mumumumumumum

Activity: Making letter waves

Learning opportunity: Making patterns by writing letters.

Early learning goal: Communication, Language and Literacy. Children should use a pencil and hold it effectively to form recognisable letters, most of which are correctly formed.

Resources: Postcards showing individual lower case letters; 30cm by 7cm strips of plain paper (Note: three strips can be cut from a piece of A4 paper); pencils and pencil-crayons; scrap paper.

Key vocabulary: Wave, names and sounds of letters.

Organisation: Small groups.

What to do: Talk about waves, the patterns they make and the way they go up and down. Look through the letter cards encouraging the children to pick out familiar ones and to say the sounds that they make. Ask the children to find a letter that looks like a wave (e.g. w) Demonstrate how to fill a strip with w to make a long wave.

Invite the children to make waves using different letters. Encourage them to form the letters correctly and to try and keep their sizes regular.

Activity: Surfboard number rhyme

Learning opportunity: Counting and subtracting using a number rhyme.

Early learning goal: Problem Solving, Reasoning and Numeracy. Children should say and use number names in order in familiar contexts. They should count reliably up to ten everyday objects. They should begin to relate … subtraction to 'taking away'.

Resources: Picture of people on surfboards.

Key vocabulary: Surf, surfboard, numbers up to ten.

Organisation: Small groups.

What to do: Show the children a picture of people on surfboards. Talk about the way surfers stretch out their arms to balance and the difficulties of riding on the waves. Pick five children to be surfers. Together count the children. Recite the surfboard rhyme encouraging the children to work out how many surfers will remain standing after a given number have 'fallen'.
5 surfers stand on boards
(5 children stand with arms outstretched)

While fishes swim below,
(Make a fish swimming motion with a hand)

A wave comes crash and _ fall in
(Choose one or more children to sit down, clap on 'crash')

Leaving __ still to go.
(Count the children still standing)

Display

Involve the children in putting up their collage tiles to make a giant grid. Encourage the children to consider which tiles should be together and which ones would look best separated. Finish the grid with a border of blue paper. On a large board display the letter pattern strips as sea waves. Put up a silhouette of a large boat on which to display the porthole views.

Week 4
Sea creatures and plants

Personal, Social and Emotional Development

- Talk about sea creatures that children have seen in real life, in films and books or on the television. Encourage the children to talk about their likes and dislikes. (PS2, 4)
- On a notice board make a frieze of a 'wishing rock pool'. Ask the children to make suggestions for wishes that would help people. Write the wishes on sea creatures cut from card. Ask the children to colour their creatures and to choose where they would like their wishes to be placed. (PS5)

Communication, Language and Literacy

- Enjoy sharing picture books that feature a sea creature (see resources for suggestions). Talk about similarities and differences in the illustrations and in the stories. (L3, 4)
- Choose a story about a sea creature that the children have not previously seen. Read the first half and then ask the children to make suggestions of what might happen next. (L4)

Problem Solving, Reasoning and Numeracy

- Look at pictures of seaweed. Talk about the different colours and shapes. Use different lengths of ribbon or crepe paper as pretend seaweed. Compare the lengths and arrange them in size order. (N9)
- Have a 'crab drive' (based on a 'beetle drive'). In turn children shake a die with numerals 1, 2 and 3. (1 = body; 2 = a pincer; 3 = a leg). Children can make a crab either by drawing or by modelling one using pipe cleaners, play-dough and matchsticks. (N3)
- Use non-fiction books or the internet to find out the sizes of whales, sharks and a variety of fish. On the playground use chalk to do a large picture of a shark or whale and compare its length with that of a child. (N4, 11)

Knowledge and Understanding of the World

- Sort a collection of different types and sizes of shells. Use non-fiction books to identify the creatures that used to live in them. (K1, 2)
- Make paper plate sea creatures (see activity opposite). (K5, 6)
- Paper plate sea creatures (see activity opposite). (K5, 6)

Physical Development

- Give the children pieces of felt cut in the shape of starfish. Encourage them to decorate the fish either by sewing with safe needles and sparkly thread or by sticking on sequins. (PD8)
- Give each child a piece of dough to turn into a sea creature. (PD8)
- Fishes in the sea game (see activity opposite). (PD1, 2)

Creative Development

- Use wax crayons to draw sea creatures and seaweed. Finish by brushing over with a wash of watery, sea-coloured paint. (C3)
- Show the children pictures or real pieces of coral. Help the children to cut bumpy pieces of coral from white or pink card. Use hole punches to provide added texture before finishing with glitter. (C3)

Activity: Paper plate sea creatures

Learning opportunity: Making paper plate sea creatures.

Early learning goal: Knowledge and Understanding of the World. Children should build and construct with a

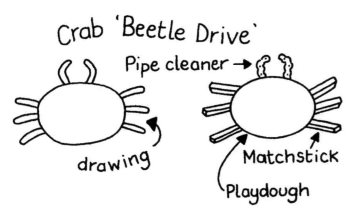

Crab 'Beetle Drive'
Pipe cleaner →
drawing
Matchstick
Playdough

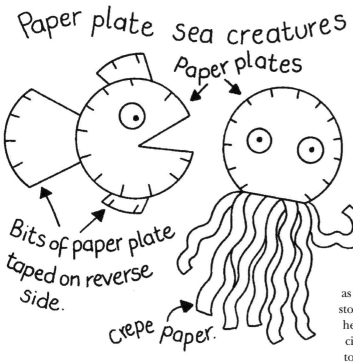

Paper plate sea creatures

Paper plates

Bits of paper plate taped on reverse side.

crepe paper.

Early learning goal: Physical Development. Children should move with confidence, imagination and in safety. They should move with control and coordination.

Resources: Large space suitable for running and for sitting on the floor.

Key vocabulary: Names for fish; tide; turn; swim.

Organisation: Large group.

What to do: Sit the children in a circle, on the floor, with their backs facing the centre of the circle. Explain that they are going to be fish in a sea. Go round the circle giving each child the name of one of four sea creatures such as salmon, cod, plaice or haddock. Tell the children a story in which fish go for a swim. When the children hear their fish name they stand and walk around the circle. Describe speeds and actions such as 'tide turn' to indicate that children should change their direction, or 'the whales came' for them to return to sit in their original places.

Display

Attach a large piece of net to the boat frieze made in week 3. Use large paperclips to display the felt fish on the net. Nearby, hang up the plate creatures at varying heights. Put up the coral pieces on windows, along with silhouettes of fish and bubbles cut from black sugar paper, to create sea themed stained glass windows.

wide range of objects, selecting appropriate resources and adapting their work where necessary. They should select the tools and techniques they need to shape, assemble and join materials they are using.

Resources: two small paper plates for each child; glue, tape, scissors, pencils, felt pens, paper scraps, wobbly eyes, pictures of fish, crepe paper, stapler.

Key vocabulary: Fish, names for available materials.

Organisation: Small groups.

What to do: Show the children pictures of fish and sea creatures. Talk about the body parts (tail, fin etc), the shapes and the colours. Show the children a paper plate and explain that they are going to turn it into a fish. Demonstrate how to cut a section out of the plate for a mouth and how to use it and pieces cut from another plate to make a tail and fins.

Show the children the available materials and pen colours. Invite them to select the ones they need for their fish. (Note: An octopus or jellyfish can be made by attaching eight strips of crepe paper to dangle from the plate. If extra plates are available plates can be stapled together to make two sided fish and these can then be hung up when finished.)

Activity: Fishes in the Sea game

Learning opportunity: Collaborating to play a game following instructions.

Week 5
Sea and beach safety

Personal, Social and Emotional Development

● Discuss ways to be safe at the seaside on sunny days such as wearing a sunhat, T-shirts with sleeves and sunscreen and not going out when your shadow is shorter than your length. Make sun safety posters. (PS2, 9)

● Talk about the roles of lifeguards and people who man lifeboats. (PS2, 3)

● Invite a child to model a cycle helmet. Explain that different activities require different types of safety equipment. Talk about what is needed for using a small boat. Explain how life jackets work. (PS1, 9)

Communication, Language and Literacy

● In a role-play home corner dress dolls to be safe in the sun. Encourage the children to role-play putting on sunscreen and to give the dolls instructions about drinking water and wearing a sunhat. (L2, 7)

● Look at picture books that have pictures of characters outside on sunny days. Encourage the children to look at what the characters are wearing and to make suggestions of what they should wear, to be safe in the sun, if they were going to the seaside. (L3)

● Making posters about being safe at the seaside and sun protection. (L17, 18, 19)

Problem Solving, Reasoning and Numeracy

● Look at pictures of flags used by lifeguards and on lifeboats. Make flags with repeating patterns on A5 paper. Tape them to plastic straws. (N10)

● Use flat shapes cut from black and orange paper to make collages of lifeboats on blue paper. Encourage the children to name the shapes that they choose to use, and also to compare the sizes. (N11)

Knowledge and Understanding of the World

● Explain that lighthouses help sailors to navigate and also, how they can give warning of dangers such as rocks. Talk about how different lighthouses have different signals. Let the children use torches to send signals in flashes of light. For safety reasons, use dim lights and remind children not to look directly into the torches. (K1)

● Use cardboard tubes and scraps of materials to make models of lighthouses. (K5)

● Investigate which colours are most visible against a blue background. Discuss what colour of swimming costume or hat would show up best in the sea. (K1, 3)

● Beach shoes (see activity opposite). (K1, 3)

Physical Development

● Take the children on an imaginary walk along a beech. Encourage the children to keep an eye on the tide, look for life guards' flags and, when safe, jump the waves. Describe a picnic on the sand, reminding the children to wear sunhats and use sunscreen. (PD1, 2)

● Circuit of beach activities (see activity opposite). (PD7)

Creative Development

● Make sunhats from large paper bowls or plates. (C3)

● Set out the role-play area as a seaside stall selling sun glasses, sunhats, T-shirts with sleeves and sunscreen. Encourage the children to be both the stall holders giving advice on sun and sea safety and, also, customers. (C5)

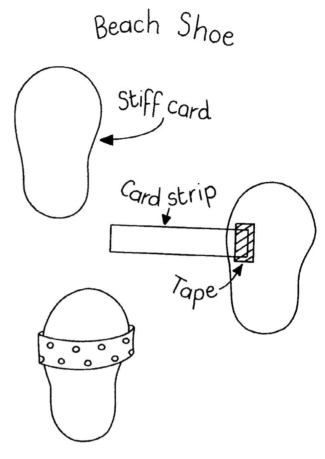

Beach Shoe

Stiff card

Card strip

Tape

Activity: Beach Shoes

Learning opportunity: Observing and making models of beach shoes.

Early learning goal: Knowledge and Understanding of the World. Children should investigate objects and materials by using all of their senses as appropriate. They should look closely at similarities (and) differences …

Resources: Examples of beach shoes; stiff card, tape, scissors, decorative materials; crayons, scissors, glue.

Key vocabulary: Names of example shoes and materials, beach.

Organisation: Small groups.

What to do: Show the children a 'flip flop'. Talk about what it is made of and the fact that it is waterproof and convenient for slipping on and off. Discuss what makes a good shoe to wear at the seaside. Examine all the shoes and encourage children to notice similarities and differences and to give reasons for whether they would be useful.

Draw around a child's foot on stiff card. Cut around the outline to make a shoe sole that is slightly bigger than the foot. Stick a strip of card on to the sole with tape to make a model of a shoe that would easily slip on and off. Explain that they are going to make models of beach shoes that would be attractive to wear. When made compare the models with an actual shoe.

Activity: Circuit of beach activities

Learning opportunity: Enjoying using bats, balls, streamers and movement activities.

Early learning goal: Physical Development. Children should use a range of small … equipment.

Resources: Picture showing children playing on a beach; bats, balls, playground chalk; ribbon streamers, bubbles and blowers; picnic rug, green flag, red flag

Key vocabulary: Names of activities.

Organisation: Large group.

What to do: Set out the activities as a circuit, ensuring that there is sufficient space for safety. In one area, chalk wave patterns for the children to jump over and walk along (paddle).

Show the children the beach picture. Talk about the kinds of activities that people like to do at beaches. Explain that it is best to swim when the tide is coming in. Tell the children that all the activities that they are going to do are ones that could take place on a beach. Demonstrate each activity and set challenges such as throwing and catching a ball ten times or batting a ball five times in the air. Explain where they can run with the streamers and how to use the chalked waves.

Remind the children of the flags used by lifeguards and the importance when at the seaside of looking out for the flags and doing as they request. Show the children a green flag and say that today it means 'use the activity'. Show a red flag and say it means 'stop what you are doing and sit down'. Enjoy using the activities moving children on after suitable intervals of time.

Display

On a table, near the role-play stall, put out lids from shoeboxes in which to display the model beach shoes and a sign saying 'shoes for sale'. Involve the children in painting boxes of different sizes to be a cliff and use them to display the lighthouses.

Week 6
Beach party

Personal, Social and Emotional Development
- Introduce the idea of the beach party. Talk about the types of activity that might be done and the kinds of clothes that the children might wear. (PS2)
- Making grass (hula) skirts (see activity opposite). (PS12)

Communication, Language and Literacy
- Write recipes for sandwiches and fruity drinks for a beach party. (L17, 18, 19)
- Make tickets for the beach party on pieces of card cut in shapes such as buckets, beach balls, fish and parasols. (L17, 18, 19)

Problem Solving, Reasoning and Numeracy
- Use large beads to make party necklaces with either repeating patterns or given numbers of different coloured beads. If possible, include some shell-shaped beads. (N1, 10)
- Talk about the need to wring out costumes after they have been used for swimming. Enjoy practising with small costumes in the water tray. Encourage the children to collect the water they wring out and to compare the amounts. (N9)

Knowledge and Understanding of the World
- Having first checked with carers for food allergies investigate fillings for beach party sandwiches such as tuna, apple and salad cream or cheese and apple. Encourage the children to think of healthy, juicy sandwiches. (K1, 3)
- Design models of rock pools. Make the models in shallow plastic dishes such as saucers for large plant pots. (K5, 6)
- Make iced fruit juice lollies. Compare the differences between liquid and frozen juice. (K3)

Physical Development
- Use balloons to play 'friendly beach volleyball'. The aim is for pairs of children to keep the balloon in the air as long as possible. (PD7)
- Enjoy making sandcastles in the sand tray. (PD7)

Creative Development
- Look at pictures or real examples of sticks of edible, stripy rock as well as rocks in interesting shapes. Explain that the way something looks often encourages people to buy it. Say that you want some ideas for ways to make fruit look interesting for a beach party. Give each child an outline of a piece of fruit. Ask them to make it into something and to colour it. For example, a banana could have a sail added to be a boat, an orange could be a head. When all the pictures are complete talk about how the designs could be done (e.g. a slice of cheese would make a good sail). (C5)
- Group net and hoop weaving (see activity opposite). (C3)

Activity: Making grass (hula) skirts

Learning opportunity: Selecting colours and resources independently to make grass skirts.

Early learning goal: Personal, Social and Emotional Development. Children should select and use activities and resources independently.

Resources: Picture or example of a grass skirt; 1.5 metre lengths of ribbon of width 1 – 2 centimetres in a variety of bright colours; metre length strips of crepe paper in a variety of colours; felt pen, music for dancing in grass skirts, stapler, tape, glue.

Key vocabulary: Names of colours, skirt.

Organisation: Whole group for the introduction, 2 children for the practical activity.

What to do: Show the children a picture of, or actual grass skirt. Talk about the colours and the way that they are worn at festivals, galas, parties and celebrations. Explain that they are going to make grass skirts that will swirl around them if they dance.

Demonstrate how to take a piece of ribbon and put on two felt pen dots to mark the central third to be the waistband. Select a piece of crepe paper and fold it over the ribbon with sufficient overlap to be able to tape, glue or staple to fix it. Invite ideas from the children for ways to secure the paper. Tell the children that to make the skirt the section of ribbon between the dots needs to be filled with hanging strips of paper.

Select pairs of children to come and make grass skirts. Encourage the children to select their own paper strips, ribbon and other resources independently. When all the skirts have been finished invite the children to wear them as they dance.

Activity: Group net and hoop weaving

Learning opportunity: Collaborating to do hoop weaving.

Early learning goal: Creative Development. Children should explore colour, texture, shape, form and space in two or three dimensions.

Resources: Large, green or blue plastic hoops with a piece of garden netting, laid on top and attached with thread; scraps of fabric, ribbon, shiny paper, parcel string etc in a range of blues and greens.

Key vocabulary: Names of colours and materials used; weave, in, out, under, over.

Organisation: Small groups.

What to do: Show the children the hoop covered with net. Tell them that the net can be used for weaving. Explain what weaving is. Demonstrate how to weave a strip of shiny blue paper. Say that together the group is going to fill the netting with weaving in materials that are similar in colour to the sea and seaweed. Invite the children to select materials to weave. When completed, hang the hoop in a safe place where it can turn.

Display

Put up one or two 'washing lines' across a notice board. Use clothes pegs to display the grass skirts and the necklaces on the lines. Place the rock pools on a table with small plastic figures for imaginative play. Use clear plastic wallets tied together with freezer bag ties or ribbon to make a beach party food recipe book. Put the book in a role-play kitchen and encourage the children to 'read' the recipes as they bake and cook.

Ribbon

Pen dots

Crepe paper

Front

Paper looped over ribbon belt & taped on.

Tape

Back - belt tied in bow.

Grass Skirts

Bringing It All Together

The Beach Party provides an excellent way to finish a topic on the sea and can also be an enjoyable, summery end to the group's year. This party could take place either inside or out depending upon the weather, available space and the number of adults at the party.

Preparation

In the week before the party ask the children to bring in plain, unwanted T-shirts. Work with individual children and use fabric crayons/pens, sequins and other decorative materials to decorate the shirts with wavy patterns, fish and boats.

Write a letter to ask parents to send in a picnic on the day of the party for their child. To fit in with the theme, some parents might cut the sandwiches in the shape of fish or put the picnics in clean, plastic, seaside buckets or plastic boxes decorated with fishy stickers. Collect large towels or picnic blankets for the picnic.

The Beach Party

Ask the children to come to the party wearing beach clothes such as shorts, hats and the decorated T-shirts. Some children might like to wear the necklaces and grass skirts that they made in Week 6. Invite parents and carers to come to the beach party and to take responsibility for some of the beach themed activities.
These might include:

- a sand tray with buckets, shells and spades;
- a water tray with boats;
- magnetic fishing;
- bats and balls;
- volley ball with balloons (aim to keep the balloon in the air);
- Frisbees (paper plates decorated by the children);
- a role-play beach souvenir and postcard shop;
- a role-play seaside with seaweed made from crepe paper; hanging paper plate fish; buckets, spades; hoops as rock pools etc;
- a Hawaiian area with calipso music, shakers, castanets and thread and tissue circles to make strings of garlands.

When the activities are set out, label each one with a fish made from card, showing the number of children who may participate in an activity at any one time.

Begin the party by splitting into small groups, each with an adult helper. Remind the children of safe procedures for a day at the beach and explain that today they must also keep with their adult. Encourage the groups to move between activities and to enjoy collaborating.

Finish the party with the picnics, iced lollies (these could be made by the children earlier in the week by freezing fruit juice) and singing sea themed songs such as 'Oh I do like to be beside the seaside' and 'A sailor went to sea, sea, sea'.

Resources

Resources to collect:
- Resources for a role-play beach souvenir shop and seaside e.g. cash register money, buckets, spades, stripy straws (to be rock), magnetic fishing game.
- Shells and pebbles
- Beach shoes
- Fabric pens
- 1.5 metre pieces of ribbon
- Strips of crepe paper in a variety of colours (to make grass skirts)
- Unwanted CDs (for artwork)
- World globe
- Sand timers
- Postcards and pictures of the sea (including the Dead Sea), beaches and people surfing.
- Edible rock or pictures of rock

Everyday resources:
- Boxes e.g. cereal packets, shoe boxes
- Variety of papers and cards e.g. sugar, tissue, silver and shiny papers, wallpaper, corrugated card, etc.
- Paint, different sized paintbrushes and a variety of paint mixing containers
- Pencils, crayons, pastels, felt pens etc.
- Glue and scissors
- Decorative and finishing materials such as sequins, foils, glitter, tinsel, shiny wool and threads, beads, pieces of textiles, parcel ribbon
- Table covers
- Malleable materials such as play-dough
- Playground chalk
- Felt squares, thread and safe needles
- Plastic straws
- Sand and water trays
- Coloured sands
- Glitter
- Dice with numerals 1, 1, 2, 2, 3, and 3

Books for children: Fiction
- *The Lighthouse Keeper's Lunch* by David Armitage (Scholastic Hippo)
- *Bright Stanley* by Matt Buckingham (Little Tiger Press)
- *Little Turtle and the Song of the Sea* by Sheridan Cain (Little Tiger Press)
- *Mister Seahorse* by Eric Carle (Puffin)
- *The Snail and the Whale* by Julia Donaldson (Little Tiger Press)
- *Fidgety Fish and Friends* by Ruth Galloway (Little Tiger Press)
- *Gilbert the Great* by Jane Clarke (Simon and Schuster)
- *To the Beach* by Thomas Docherty (Templar Publishing)
- *Splash!* by Jane Hissey (Red Fox)
- *The Rainbow Fish* by Marcus Pfister (North-South Books)
- *The Bear in the Cave* by Michael Rosen (Bloomsbury Paperbacks)

Non-fiction
- *Dolphins and Whales* by Caroline Bingham (Dorling Kindersley Ltd)
- *Deep Blue Sea* by Richard Ferguson (Dorling Kindersley Ltd)
- *My First Book of Ocean Life* by Alison Howard (Ticktock Media Ltd)
- *Sea Creatures* by Sue Malyan (Dorling Kindersley Ltd)
- *Mad about Sharks* by Deborah Murrell (Ladybird Books Ltd)

Poems and Rhymes
- *Commotion in the Ocean* by Giles Andreae (Orchard Books)
- *Five Little Monkeys* by Zita Newcome (Walker Books)

Resources for planning
- *The Early Years Foundation Stage Setting the Standards for Learning, Development and Care for children from birth to* (Department for Education and Skills)

five

Collecting Evidence of Children's Learning

Monitoring children's development is an important task. Keeping a record of children's achievements, interests and learning styles will help you to see progress and will draw attention to those who are having difficulties for some reason. If a child needs additional professional help, such as speech therapy, your records will provide valuable evidence.

Records should be the result of collaboration between group leaders, parents and carers. Parents should be made aware of your record keeping policies when their child joins your group. Show them the type of records you are keeping and make sure they understand that they have an opportunity to contribute. As a general rule, your records should form an open document. Any parent should have access to records relating to his or her child. Take regular opportunities to talk to parents about children's progress. If you have formal discussions regarding children about whom you have particular concerns, a dated record of the main points should be kept.

Keeping it manageable

Records should be helpful in informing group leaders, adult helpers and parents and always be for the benefit of the child. The golden rule is to make them simple, manageable and useful.

Observations will basically fall into three categories:
- **Spontaneous records:** Sometimes you will want to make a note of observations as they happen, for example, a child is heard counting cars accurately during a play activity, or is seen to play collaboratively for the first time.

- **Planned observations:** Sometimes you will plan to make observations of children's developing skills in their everyday activities. Using the learning opportunity identified for an activity will help you to make appropriate judgements about children's capabilities and to record them systematically.

To collect information:
- talk to children about their activities and listen to their responses;
- listen to children talking to each other;
- observe children's work such as early writing, drawings, paintings and 3D models. (Keeping photocopies or photographs is useful.)

Sometimes you may wish to set up 'one off' activities for the purposes of monitoring development. Some pre-school groups, for example, ask children to make a drawing of themselves at the beginning of each term to record their progressing skills in both co-ordination and observation. Do not attempt to make records after every activity!

- **Reflective observations:** It is useful to spend regular time reflecting on the children's progress. Aim to make some brief comments about each child every week.

Informing your planning

Collecting evidence about children's progress is time consuming and it is important that it is useful. When you are planning, use the information you have collected to help you to decide what learning opportunities you need to provide next for children. For example, a child who has poor pencil or brush control will benefit from more play with dough or construction toys to build the strength of hand muscles.

Example of recording chart

Name: Helena Shepherdson		D.O.B. 17.5.04		Date of entry: 17.9.08	
Term	**Personal, Social and Emotional Development**	**Communication, Language and Literacy**	**Problem Solving, Reasoning and Numeracy**	**Knowledge and Understanding of the World**	**Physical Development**	**Creative Development**
ONE	Happy to say good-bye to mother. Enjoys both independent and collaborative play. 30.9.08 LBS	Enjoying listening to and retelling stories – excellent memory for details and phrases. Can write first name and simple CVC words. Good pencil grip. 2.10.08 CCM	Is able to say and recognise numbers to ten and to count accurately five objects. Enjoyed subtracting in the Surfers Rhyme. 7.11.08 EHL	Very eager to ask questions always wants to know 'Why?' Keen to look for sea and holiday places on the globe. 16.10.08 LSS	Very flexible. Can balance on one leg. Loved miming being a surfer. Good at aiming. 9.10.08 SJS	Enjoys painting and particularly when mixing own colours. Good at large scale weaving. Not keen to get hands messy. Tuneful voice and good memory for words – loved singing sea songs. 22.10.08 REL
TWO						
THREE						

Skills overview of six-week plan

Week	Topic Focus	Personal, Social and Emotional Development	Communication, Language and Literacy	Problem Solving, Reasoning and Numeracy	Knowledge and Understanding of the World	Physical Development	Creative Development
1	Sea detective	Showing interest; Speaking; Maintaining attention	Listening; Using phonic knowledge to write words; Collecting rhyming words; Sharing books	Counting; Sorting; Comparing; Using positional language	Making observations; Comparing; Finding out about and identifying features in the natural world	Moving with control, co-ordination, and imagination in safety; Recognising body changes after activity.	Collage; Painting; Using pastels and chalks
2	Sand, shells and pebbles	Showing interest; Sharing feelings and showing sensitivity to others	Listening; Writing; Collaborating to write a poem; Practising letter formation	Recognising and describing shapes; Making patterns; Sorting; Counting	Comparing; Describing; Observing	Handling objects with control and safely; Using small equipment and malleable materials	Painting; Sticking; Collage
3	On the sea	Considering consequences; Showing interest and feelings	Hearing and saying sounds Using phonic knowledge to write words; Making up stories; Practising letter formation	Counting; Using positional language; Developing awareness of subtraction	Observing; Comparing; Asking questions; Selecting tools and techniques; Constructing	Moving with control and co-ordination; Balancing	Collage; Painting; Singing; Dancing
4	Sea creatures and plants	Speaking; Initiating ideas; Considering consequences; Showing feelings	Speaking; Listening; Responding to stories	Counting; Recognising numbers; Comparing lengths	Comparing Investigating; Constructing; Selecting materials, techniques and tools	Moving with control, co-ordination, imagination and in safety; Using small equipment and malleable materials	Singing; Wax-resist painting
5	Sea and beach safety	Being confident to try new activities; Maintain attention; Understand what is right and wrong and why	Responding to a story; Writing; Speaking; Listening; Role-play	Making patterns; Recognising shapes	Investigating; Constructing; Observing; Talking; Selecting tools and technique	Moving with imagination; Using small equipment; Throwing, and aiming	Cutting and sticking; Role-play
6	Beach party	Being confident to try new activities; Being independent	Using phonic knowledge to write words	Comparing; Making patterns	Investigating; Comparing; Constructing	Using small equipment	Drawing; Weaving

Planning for Learning through The Sea

Home links

The theme of the sea lends itself to useful links with children's homes and families. Through working together children and adults will gain respect for each other and build comfortable and confident relationships.

Establishing Partnerships
- Keep parents informed about the topic of 'the sea' and the themes for each week. By understanding the work of the group, parents will enjoy the involvement of contributing ideas, time and resources.
- Photocopy the parent's page for each child to take home.
- Invite friends, child minders and families to share in the beach party.

Visiting Enthusiasts
- Invite parents and carers to talk about times they went on holidays to a beach when they were children. Ask them to describe activities they carried out and to talk about what they wore.
- Invite parents who enjoy craft to plan and run a safe activity about shells. This might include decorating boxes, making jewellery, making animals with shells etc.

Resource Requests
- Ask parents to donate items for a seaside display such as buckets, spades, sand moulds etc.
- Encourage recycling by asking for unwanted books that fit in with any of the weekly themes.

The Beach Party
- Extra adults are always useful at occasions such as the beach party. Involve parents and carers in running the circuit of beach themed activities. Encourage them to work in role and to join in with the wearing of beach clothes and in the picnic. Before the party, tell the children that the parents and carers will be their guests and help them to consider how to look after guests.